POLITICAL PROFILES
NANCY PELOSI

Political Profiles
Nancy Pelosi

Sandra H. Shichtman

MORGAN
REYNOLDS
PUBLISHING

Greensboro, North Carolina

POLITICAL PROFILES

Barack Obama
Hillary Clinton
John McCain
Nancy Pelosi
Al Gore
Rudy Giuliani
Arnold Schwarzenegger

POLITICAL PROFILES: NANCY PELOSI

Copyright © 2008 by Sandra H. Shichtman

Library of Congress Cataloging-in-Publication Data

Shichtman, Sandra H.
  Political profiles : Nancy Pelosi / by Sandra H. Shichtman.
    p. cm.
  Includes bibliographical references and index.
  ISBN-13: 978-1-59935-049-3
  ISBN-10: 1-59935-049-1
  1. Pelosi, Nancy, 1940---Juvenile literature. 2. Women legislators--United
States--Biography--Juvenile literature. 3. Legislators--United States--Biography-
-Juvenile literature. 4. United States. Congress. House--Biography--Juvenile
literature. 5. United States. Congress. House--Speakers--Biography--Juvenile
literature. I. Title.
  E840.8.P37S54 2007
  328.73092--dc22
  [B]

                              2007023576

Printed in the United States of America
First Edition

*For my dear friend Eli Indenbaum, who has
left this world but will never leave my heart*

Contents

Nancy Pelosi
(Courtesy of AP Images/Charles Dharapak)

one

A Noble Calling

J anuary 4, 2007, fell on a Thursday, but it was hardly
an ordinary Thursday in the Congress of the United
States. The Democratic Party had taken control of both
the Senate and the House of Representatives as a result of
the elections the previous November. On January 4th, the
110th Congress gathered in Washington, D.C. to swear in
their leaders.

The floor was filled with the members of both houses.
The galleries were packed with their families and friends as
well as invited members of the public. Representative Nancy
Pelosi of California was sworn in as Speaker of the House,
the most important position in American government following the president and the vice-president. For Representative
Pelosi it was the culmination of a long political career.

Dressed in a suit the color of eggplant and with a strand of
pearls around her neck, Nancy Pelosi walked to the rostrum.
Surrounded by a group of congressional children, including

On January 4, 2007, Pelosi was sworn in as the first woman Speaker of the House. *(Courtesy of AP Images/Pablo Martinez Monsivais)*

her own grandchildren, Pelosi took the oath of office. She made history that day, shattering the traditional "marble ceiling" that prevented women from reaching positions of top leadership in Congress.

In accepting the position, Pelosi told the Congress and the American people, "This is an historic moment. It's an historic moment for the Congress. It's an historic moment for the women of America. It is a moment for which we have waited for over 200 years."

Nancy Pelosi had come a long way from her beginnings in Baltimore, Maryland, but she still retained the values she had learned as a child living at home. Her father, Thomas J. D'Alesandro, Jr., was born in Baltimore on August 1, 1903.

As a boy, Thomas D'Alesandro sold newspapers on the streets of Baltimore to earn money. He attended Catholic schools and then worked in the insurance business. He dropped into the local Democratic headquarters whenever he could and, during election time rang the doorbells of voters and gave out handbills urging voters to elect specific Democratic candidates. When he decided to enter politics himself, he joined the Democratic Party, the party of the poor and working class.

He saw firsthand the problems immigrants faced. They needed to find jobs, learn to speak English, get an education, and become American citizens. Early in his political career, D'Alesandro began to help these immigrant citizens assimilate into the American culture and economy.

In 1926, D'Alesandro, later known as Old Tommy or Tommy the Elder, was elected to the Maryland House of Delegates. He walked into the chamber on his first day in office dressed in a gray suit, a polka-dot tie, patent-leather

Pelosi's father, Thomas D'Alesandro, shakes hands with naval captain William M. Cole while serving as mayor of Baltimore. *(Courtesy of Naval Historical Center Archives)*

shoes, and a derby hat. The polka-dot tie became his good luck charm and he wore it regularly after that.

D'Alesandro later served five terms as a U.S. congressman. In 1947, he was elected mayor of Baltimore and served three terms. By that time he was married and the father of six children.

Seven-year-old Nancy stood beside her father as he took the oath of office. She recalled an incident that took place when her parents took her to a voting place for the first time. A worker for the Republican Party saw little Nancy and gave her a toy elephant (the elephant is the symbol of the Republican Party). Nancy quickly gave it back. "He thinks I don't know what this is. I was offended. In our family, it

Nancy Pelosi as a young girl with her family

was about whose side are you on; the whole idea of working for families and the opportunity they had," she explained later. She realized, even when she was very young, that the Democratic Party was *her* party.

People in his old neighborhood expected the new mayor to move his family into a better neighborhood. But Old Tommy refused to move. "It's not where you live, it's how you live," he said. The mayor believed in giving a hand up to those who were down. Throughout his career, he worked hard for working-class people and never forgot his own working-class roots.

Old Tommy was a New Deal Democrat. The New Deal was the name President Franklin Delano Roosevelt gave to a series of federal programs he authorized between the years 1933 and 1937. The United States was in the midst of the Great Depression and people had lost their jobs and could not feed their families. The New Deal programs offered help, including emergency relief programs to feed the hungry and work relief programs to get Americans working again. There were also agricultural programs to help American farmers. Politicians who were considered New Deal Democrats, like Tommy D'Alesandro, believed that the government should help people who needed it.

D'Alesandro had married Annunciata Lombardi, Nancy's mother, in 1928. Annunciata, who was always known as Nancy, was born in Italy in 1909. She grew up in Baltimore's Little Italy, a neighborhood of about twelve square blocks located close to the harbor, where many Italian immigrants had settled to work in the port, loading and unloading the ships.

Like most of their neighbors, the Lombardis sent their daughter to school at St. Leo's Roman Catholic Church, the same school Nancy's daughter later attended. Before her marriage, Nancy Lombardi attended law school, but, like many women of her generation, she gave up her plans for higher education in order to marry, settle down, and raise a family.

She and her husband had five sons—Thomas III (who later served one term as mayor of Baltimore), Nicholas, Hector, Joseph, and Franklin (who was named for President Franklin Delano Roosevelt). Finally, a daughter was born on March 26, 1940.

The D'Alesandros were staunch Democrats and named their youngest son after President Franklin Delano Roosevelt (above).

Word of the little girl's birth spread quickly in Little Italy, the close-knit working class Italian neighborhood where the D'Alesandros lived. The D'Alesandros named their daughter Nancy Patricia. But, to everyone, she was always known as "Little Nancy."

The D'Alesandros were devout Catholics who raised their children in the Catholic religion. They were proud of their Italian heritage and instilled that pride in Little Nancy and her brothers. They were also staunch Democrats who taught their children that public service was a noble calling.

In addition to caring for her household and growing family, Mrs. D'Alesandro was active in her husband's political career. She organized groups of women to help in her husband's reelection campaigns. She invited them to her home, where they met on a regular basis to plan rallies and to work the political precincts. Mrs. D'Alesandro also gave spaghetti dinners to raise money for the Democratic Party and its candidates who were running for office.

Nancy D'Alesandro was typical of women of her era. During World War II, men were drafted into the army and sent overseas to fight in Germany and Japan. American women took over the jobs the men had left behind. After the war, the women returned to their homes, but they had gotten a taste of being powerful and would not give it up easily. More women went to college and many others continued to work and to become interested and involved in politics. Mrs. D'Alesandro was one of those women.

Mrs. D'Alesandro was a disciplinarian who maintained order in her home. It was a trait that she passed along to her daughter. It would prove valuable to Little Nancy when she managed her own home and family and, later, as she entered the world of politics.

Little Nancy saw her mother as a role model, inspiring her to aim high and achieve. It was obvious to her, even when she was a child, that Mrs. D'Alesandro liked people and enjoyed doing things for them and in their behalf. All the D'Alesandro children, including Little Nancy, grew up with their mother's values of service to other people, which they incorporated into their own lives.

The D'Alesandro children were enlisted in helping their father's political career. Their brick row house at 245 Albemarle Street, at the corner of Fawn Street, was always open to visitors and constituents. People came to ask the mayor for help and he never turned anyone down. Nancy's eldest brother, Thomas, recalled in an interview, "During the leaner years, we had in our back room the equivalent of a soup kitchen."

All the children took turns sitting at a desk that was set up in the front room of the house. They wrote down the name of each person who came to ask for help in a notebook which was known as the "favor file." They wrote down what the people asked for and what the mayor did to help them.

"Our whole lives were politics. If you entered the house, it was always campaign time, and if you went into the living room, it was always constituent time," Little Nancy recalled years later.

She added, "Our lives were about campaigns" during most of the year. Only during Christmas or Easter was there a time "when you could walk into our home and you were not given a placard or a bumper sticker or a brochure to distribute."

During their father's reelection campaigns, the D'Alesandro children stuffed envelopes with letters appealing for votes. The letters included reminders of what favors the mayor had done for them in the past and suggested that they could return the favor by voting for the mayor. It was here that young Nancy learned how the game of politics was played.

Her brother Thomas remembered, "We'd call people up and say, 'Mrs. So-and-So, we did this favor for you and now my father is running for reelection. We'd like to borrow your car to get people out to vote' or 'you can come lick stamps' or 'you can organize a coffee klatch'."

Being the youngest child in the family was both a blessing and a hindrance for Nancy. "I was pampered in the fact that I had five older brothers . . .," she explained years later. "I wanted to be independent. And they were always . . . 'Oh, you can't do this, you can't do that.' Telling me all the things I couldn't do." She learned early in life how to get what she wanted from her brothers. Later, that would help her get what she wanted in the masculine world of politics.

The D'Alesandro family worshipped at St. Leo's Roman Catholic Church two blocks from their house. When Nancy was of school age, her parents enrolled her in school at St. Leo's. Dressed in her school uniform, Nancy went to school each morning.

She graduated from St. Leo's in 1954 and went on to high school at the all-girls Institute of Notre Dame several blocks farther away on North Aisquith Street. There Nancy's interest in politics continued to develop. While she was in high school, she took her friends to hear Massachusetts senator John F. Kennedy give a talk about his book, *Profiles in Courage.* It had been published in 1956 and told the stories of senators who had the courage to go against popular opinion to do what they thought was right for the people of the United States. Kennedy would later become president of the United States.

In 1958, Nancy enrolled at Trinity College (now Trinity University) in Washington, D.C., where she majored in political science. She was active in several on-campus clubs, including the political affairs and international relations clubs. "Let me just say, I loved Trinity College," she said later. "It was an absolute joy to go there. For me it was a break from politics. My family was steeped in politics and so it was a nice break. Yes, we were in Washington, D.C., so I was active with the College Democrats. All of us, we felt very nurtured at Trinity . . ." She was also active in the dramatic society and the French club.

Nancy lived on-campus for four years until she graduated from Trinity in 1962. It was the first time she had been away from home. She met many young women at Trinity, some of whom are still her friends today.

She also met Paul Pelosi, a student at Georgetown University in Washington, D.C. Shortly after she graduated from college, Nancy D'Alesandro and Paul Pelosi were married.

two
Marriage and Family Come First

After their marriage in 1963, Nancy and Paul Pelosi moved to New York, where they lived for six years. Paul Pelosi began his career in banking, and Nancy, much as her mother had before, stayed at home to raise their children. During the years they lived in New York, the Pelosis had four children. Their first child, a daughter, was born in 1964. They named her Nancy Corrine. Christine was born in 1966 and Jacqueline was born in 1967. A son, Paul, Jr., was born in 1969.

In 1967, Nancy Pelosi's brother Thomas, known as Tommy the Younger, was elected mayor of Baltimore. He served one term as mayor.

Two years later, the Pelosi family moved west to California, where they settled in Paul's hometown of San Francisco. They moved into a large and attractive house in the Presidio Terrace section of the city. By the time the Pelosis got to San Francisco, Paul had made money as a banker and real

Paul and Nancy Pelosi *(Courtesy of AP Images/Gerald Herbert)*

estate developer. Through Paul Pelosi's business contacts, they made many friends among the wealthy and influential people in San Francisco.

The year after their arrival, Nancy and Paul Pelosi had their fifth, and last, child, a daughter they named Alexandra. Nancy Pelosi soon was involved with the Democratic Party in San Francisco, and began to introduce her wealthy friends to important people in California's Democratic Party.

Paul Pelosi described his wife's first years in California: "Well, we end up in San Francisco. We raise our five children and when the children were in school all day, then [Nancy] started doing volunteer stuff."

Her volunteer work with the Democratic Party was important to Pelosi. But, raising her children came first. She drove them to school and to after-school activities. She expected that they would do their best. "We were always expected to make sure our homework was done; and that we were prepared for what we did. She [Mom] would always say, 'Proper preparation prevents poor performance'," recalled her daughter, Christine.

While her children were young, Pelosi helped the Democratic Party with get-out-the-vote drives and attended campaign strategy sessions. She often brought her children along, dressing them in clothing of matching colors so she could always find them among the crowds of people. She also put them to work in the same way that her father had involved young Nancy and her brothers in his campaigns.

"We five kids would have a little assembly line system," said Christine. "One of us would stuff envelopes, one would seal, one stamp and so on."

The Pelosis made contributions of large sums of money to the Democratic Party. Nancy Pelosi also became very skillful at raising money for local Democratic candidates. Her generosity and her ability to raise money brought her to the attention of local lawmakers. Among the many people she became friendly with were the Burtons—John, his brother Phil, and Phil's wife, Sala.

John Burton (left) stands with California state treasurer Phil Angelides. Burton was instrumental in convincing Pelosi to run for the congressional seat left vacant by his sister-in-law's death. *(Courtesy of AP Images/Marcio Jose Sanchez)*

John Burton, a lawyer, was a member of the California State Assembly by the time the Pelosis brought their family to California. He later became a state senator and then represented his district in the House of Representatives in Washington, D.C.

His older brother Phillip was a member of the House of Representatives from California's Fifth Congressional District, the same congressional district in which the Pelosi's house was located. He had been elected in 1964 and served in office until his death in 1983. When Phil Burton first saw the Pelosis' large and beautiful house in the wealthy neighborhood of Presidio Terrace, he told Nancy Pelosi, "We'll use this [house] for fundraising." Pelosi gave many fundraising events in her home during Phil Burton's reelection campaigns.

While he served in the House of Representatives, Phil Burton helped pass many important pieces of legislation, including bills to establish Supplemental Security Income (SSI) for Americans who were elderly or disabled. He also worked to compensate coal miners who contracted black lung disease from working in the mines, to increase the minimum wage for all workers, and to make it possible for men and women who went out on strike for higher wages and benefits to receive food stamps from the government while they were out of work. He also helped to increase the size and number of national parks in the United States.

Phil Burton was a progressive legislator who was committed to helping people. He saw in Nancy Pelosi someone who shared the same commitment to progressive values that he had. From her work as a volunteer with the Democratic Party, he also saw that she had a clear sense of how politics worked and how to turn those values into law—skills she had learned from her father.

When John Burton retired from office in 1982, he asked her to run for his old office. She turned him down because her children were small and she believed that they needed their mother at home. "It was important for me to be there for them," she later told an interviewer.

While her children grew up, Pelosi still did not think about running for office on her own. She was satisfied to continue to give fundraising parties to provide money for local Democratic candidates. She was an excellent hostess with an endearing personality that made people eager to attend her parties and dinners. She became a very capable fundraiser, raising large sums of money. As she became more widely known, she began to move up the ranks of the state and national Democratic Party. In 1976, Pelosi joined the Democratic National Committee when she was selected as a Democratic National Committeewoman from California, a position she served in for the next twenty years.

That year, California governor Jerry Brown ran in the primary elections as a candidate for president of the United States. When the primary election was held in Maryland, Nancy Pelosi worked hard for his candidacy there. In the end, thanks in part to Pelosi's help, Brown won the Maryland primary. However, he didn't win the Democratic nomination, which went to Jimmy Carter of Georgia. In 1977, Pelosi served as northern chairwoman for the California Democratic Party.

In 1980 Republican Ronald Reagan, the former governor of California, was elected president. The Republican Party also dominated California politics. The California Democrats knew they needed to work hard to elect their own members in the next election. The California Democratic Party elected Nancy Pelosi as their state chairwoman in 1981. By then, she had developed a reputation for being able to get things done.

Three years later, in 1984, the Democratic National Presidential Convention was held in San Francisco. Pelosi helped in the effort to get the Democrats to come to the convention. She gave parties in her Presidio Terrace home that were designed to recruit volunteers and was chosen to be chairwoman of the host committee. Later that year, she became chairwoman of the Democratic National Committee.

Due in part to Pelosi's efforts, San Francisco was chosen to host the Democratic National Convention in 1984. In this photo, Pelosi celebrates with San Francisco deputy mayor Hadley Roth after hearing the good news. *(Courtesy of AP Images/Scott Stewart)*

She had finally emerged as an important person on the national level for the Democratic Party.

Pelosi's friend and mentor, Phil Burton, died while in office in 1983. A special election was held to elect someone to serve out the remainder of his term and his widow Sala ran for the office and won.

In the meantime, Pelosi continued to serve the Democratic Party on the national level. She became finance chairwoman for the National Democratic Senatorial Campaign Committee, providing money for candidates running on the Democratic ticket for the Senate in races across the country. Pelosi earned the appreciation of her party for helping the Democrats win back the seats they'd lost in the Senate.

In late 1986, Sala Burton became ill with cancer. Although she was sworn into office in January 1987, she knew that she was too ill to withstand the rigors of another electoral campaign. She decided she would not run for reelection when her term in office was over in 1988.

Early in 1987, as she lay dying in the hospital, Sala asked her brother-in-law, John Burton, to visit her. She told him she wanted to ask Nancy Pelosi for a favor. She wanted Pelosi to run for her seat after she died.

However, her brother-in-law heard Sala Burton speak only the name, *Nancy*, and misunderstood to whom Sala referred. He thought she wanted Nancy Walker, then a member of San Francisco's Board of Supervisors, to run for her seat. It never occurred to him that his sister-in-law had chosen Nancy Pelosi to succeed her. At the time, Pelosi was little known outside Democratic Party circles. Even voters in her own Congressional district did not know her.

John Burton was surprised and a bit skeptical about Pelosi's ability to be a candidate for an elective office. While she was noted for her fundraising ability, she had no experience as a candidate. But it was Pelosi's talent and commitment to Democratic causes that appealed to Sala Burton.

Nancy Pelosi's life had come to a crossroads. She could stay where she was and continue to help other Democratic candidates win elections. Or, she could head in a different direction.

three
Running for
Congress

*T*he year 1987 was a crucial one for Nancy Pelosi. Before Sala Burton asked her to succeed her as representative from the Fifth Congressional District (in 1993, it became the Eighth Congressional District), Pelosi had been content to work for the election of other Democrats. "I have never not participated in a campaign, no matter how little my babies were, if I was wheeling them in a carriage or carrying them in my stomach," she said.

Now the Pelosi children were older. Their youngest daughter, Alexandra, was a senior in high school. It was time for Pelosi to think about what she wanted to do with the next years of her life. Suddenly, Sala Burton's request made a great deal of sense to Pelosi. She agreed to run for the office. "I really believe Sala is going to get better," she announced. "I will seek her seat in 1988 if she does not run."

Despite never having run for office before, Pelosi believed she could win. Her self-confidence was nurtured as a child

back home in Baltimore. Her mother, herself a strong and confident woman, instilled self-confidence in her only daughter. She told the young Nancy that she could do anything she set out to do, as long as she was willing to work hard to achieve her goals. Being in the public eye and dealing with constituents during her father's three terms in office as mayor of Baltimore added to Pelosi's self-confidence.

When she met with Sala Burton, Sala assured her the time had come to stop helping other Democrats run for office and to run for office herself. "Sala told me 'You'll be satisfied to work on the issues yourself, versus getting others to work on them. And you'll be able to make change'," Pelosi recalled the conversation later.

Sala Burton died in a Washington, D.C., hospital of colon cancer on February 1, 1987. She was sixty-one years old. California law requires that an election to fill a vacant seat be held on a Tuesday between 112 and 119 days after the governor officially proclaims that it is needed. In this case, the election would have to be held in early June. But, first, a primary election needed to be held eight weeks prior to the general election.

The Pelosis moved from their Presidio Terrace home to one they rented in a neighborhood of San Francisco known as Pacific Heights. They did this to make certain there would be no dispute as to whether or not the candidate lived in the congressional district she wanted to represent.

She entered the special primary election as one of fourteen candidates from different political parties, including Democrats, Republicans, independents, and candidates from minor political parties. Under California law, if any one candidate wins a majority of the votes in the primary, there

Pelosi announces her candidacy for the 5th Congressional District seat during this 1987 press conference. *(Courtesy of AP Images/Jim Gerberich)*

would be no need for a general election. A candidate is said to receive the majority of the votes if he or she received 50 percent of the vote plus one more vote.

Pelosi participated in a forum with other candidates. The candidates answered questions from people in the audience. She spoke about environmental and AIDS-related issues, two concerns of a majority of the people of San Francisco. She took a stand on a local issue—the docking of a battleship, the *Missouri*—in San Francisco harbor. Those in favor of having the *Missouri* in San Francisco talked about the jobs it would create for San Franciscans. Those who opposed the docking did so on the grounds that the *Missouri* carried nuclear missiles. Pelosi adopted a middle-of-the-road position. She wanted to see the *Missouri* in San Francisco, but without its nuclear missiles. She defended herself against claims that because she was a wealthy woman, she would be out of touch with her constituents, many of whom were poor.

She was also accused of being "fuzzy" on the issues. To this accusation, Pelosi retorted, "What are the issues? Well, I'll do a great job. I love the city of San Francisco. And I come from the urban tradition."

Pelosi's main opponent in that primary election was a San Francisco supervisor, Harry Britt, also a Democrat. Britt was openly homosexual and was convinced that San Francisco's large homosexual and lesbian population would vote him into office.

Britt looked for anything negative in Nancy Pelosi's background that he could use to give him an edge. He even hired a private detective to look into the business dealings of the Pelosi family. The detective discovered that the tenants in an apartment building on San Francisco's Lake Street owned by Paul Pelosi had once had a rent dispute with their landlord. But Paul Pelosi had sold that apartment building before his wife announced her intention to run for office. Despite the fact that the Pelosi family no longer owned the property, Harry Britt publicized the story.

During her first campaign for office, Pelosi employed many of the same tactics her father used during his campaigns. *(Courtesy of AP Images/Paul Sakuma)*

In polls taken before the primary election, Pelosi led the other candidates for most of the campaign period. She was ahead of Britt by about a two-to-one margin. A Pelosi supporter attributed Britt's poor poll numbers to the fact that he spent most of his time attacking Pelosi and not enough time talking to the voters about his positions on important issues. Pelosi was also endorsed by officeholders who were popular with the voters of San Francisco, including San Francisco's mayor, Dianne Feinstein, Senator Alan Cranston, California's lieutenant governor Leo McCarthy, and Assembly Speaker Willie Brown.

In her campaign speeches, Pelosi emphasized her fundraising and leadership experience in the Democratic Party. She maintained that she would be the best candidate for voters to send to Washington because of her national connections. She would be able to do more for her constituents in Washington than any of the other candidates, who were only known locally.

She refused to run a negative campaign. Instead, her campaign was similar to the ones she had watched her father run in Baltimore. When Thomas D'Alesandro ran for the office of mayor of Baltimore, he had volunteers contact potential voters, convince them to vote for him, and arranged for them to be driven to the voting site if necessary. Pelosi's campaign was an updated version of her father's.

Her campaign manager hired two professional campaign organizers who put together a voter turnout program. They identified groups of people they felt supported Pelosi and would vote for her, mailed campaign literature to them, and targeted them in their television advertising. Then they made certain that those people came out and voted.

On April 7, 1987, the voters in the fifth district of San Francisco cast their ballots for the candidate they believed should complete Sala Burton's term in the House of Representatives. Because a majority of the registered voters in the district were Democrats, it was almost a certainty that a Democratic candidate would win.

Pelosi won the primary election by a narrow margin of approximately 2,000 votes. "I am very happy and I owe it all to my campaign organization, which worked very hard to target our vote and turn it out," she said after all the votes had been counted.

Because she did not get a majority of the votes, Pelosi had to run against the top vote-getter for the Republicans, Harriet Ross. Prior to the beginning of the run-off campaign, she met with reporters. She told them that if the voters sent her to Washington, she would work hard to convince Congress to increase funding for AIDS research and programs. "I would try to impress on Congress to have a change in attitude, to treat AIDS as an earthquake in San Francisco," she said. At the time, San Francisco had more people with AIDS than any other city in the U.S.

Paul Pelosi joined Leo McCarthy and John Burton to manage his wife's campaign. He helped raise money—more than $1 million—and involved himself in knowing the details about how the campaign was being run, and attended meetings to be certain that the campaign ran properly.

Sala Burton had asked her brother-in-law to help Pelosi get elected. He later recalled his conversation with Sala: "...she launches into this thing like she's nominating a president, that she's (Pelosi) smart, she's tough, she's good on the issues, she's organized, she understands..." John Burton understood then that Sala had given her selection of Pelosi a great deal of thought, knew her abilities, and felt Pelosi was the right person to succeed her.

Pelosi's brother, Thomas D'Alesandro, the former mayor of Baltimore, flew to San Francisco to see whether his sister needed any assistance. He saw that she was in excellent hands and it was obvious that she would win the election. She had a very capable organization that would introduce her to the voters and make certain that her name and face were recognizable by election day.

The election was held on June 2, 1987. Although it was a mild, sunny day, only 39 percent of eligible voters went to the polls. Even so, Pelosi won by an overwhelming majority of 62 percent in the heavily Democratic fifth district of San Francisco.

Pelosi had been expected to win the election. Sala Burton had endorsed her before she died in February. Sala's endorsement carried a lot of weight with voters, who thought highly of her, her husband Phillip, and her brother-in-law, John. Pelosi recognized and appreciated the importance of Sala's endorsement. "Nothing was more significant than the endorsement of Sala Burton, and we had an organization to match the endorsement," she said when the ballots had all been counted.

"My top priorities will be cutting off aid to the contras and increasing funding and education efforts for AIDS," she promised. The contras were a group of rebels fighting against the Sandinista National Liberation Front (called the Sandinistas) in Nicaragua, a country in Central America. The Sandinistas were members of a political party that was founded on communist principles that had seized power in 1979.

The Sandinistas aligned themselves with the Soviet Union, and the United States and the Soviet Union were enemies. When the contras began to fight the Sandinistas, the U.S. supported them. But the contras did not only fight the army of the Sandinistas. They also attacked civilians, farmers, workers, and anyone else they suspected of supporting the government. In March 1987, President Ronald Reagan had asked Congress for $105 million to aid the contras. Nancy Pelosi opposed giving them the aid.

Pelosi was strongly opposed to funding the contras, a Nicaraguan rebel group, and promised to vote against supplying them with U.S. aid. *(Courtesy of AP Images/Iran-Contra Committee HO)*

Pelosi is being sworn into office as her father (middle) and others look on. *(Courtesy of AP Images/Rep. Pelosi's Office)*

She was sworn into office on June 9, 1987. Nancy Pelosi was on her way to the nation's capital, Washington, D.C.

four
Representative Pelosi of California

Soon after she was sworn into office, Nancy Pelosi had to begin planning her next election. She had to run in November 1988 for a full term in the House of Representatives. She ran and won overwhelmingly with 76 percent of the votes in the heavily Democratic district.

Members of Congress are usually invited by their leadership to serve on one or more committees. Pelosi was appointed to the House Committee on Appropriations, an important committee that tells the government how much money each of its departments can spend. It has many subcommittees that appropriates money for areas such as agriculture, defense, transportation, and education. Each subcommittee allots money for one segment of the federal government.

The members of the Appropriations Committee have a lot of power. They decide which districts can get money from the federal government for projects, which means job opportunities for constituents in those districts. A committee member

During her tenure as congresswoman, Pelosi served on a number of important committees, including the House Intelligence Committee and the Ethics Committee. *(Courtesy of AP Images/Justin Sullivan)*

can funnel money to his or her district or can give money to the districts of other representatives they want to influence.

During her first decade in Washington, D.C., Pelosi focused her attention on three major issues that were important to the people in her district. San Francisco has a large population of homosexual men and women, and many of her constituents suffered from HIV and AIDS. From her first term on, Pelosi urged that more money be allotted to fund research and treatment for the virus and disease. She also supported efforts to find a vaccine.

Pelosi (far right) watches as President Clinton signs the Ryan White
Care Act, which allocates funds and services for people with AIDS.
(Courtesy of Chuck Kennedy/AFP/Getty Images)

One of the first things she accomplished after coming to
Washington was the creation of the Housing Opportunities
for People with AIDS program. She worked on other HIV/
AIDS-related issues, such as expanding access to Medicaid,
the government's medical insurance program for the poor, for
people living with HIV and AIDS. She also increased access

to health insurance for people with disabilities by ensuring that their health care coverage continued.

In 1992, Pelosi became chairwoman of the Democratic National Convention's platform committee. The platform committee decides on the party's agenda for the upcoming election.

After the 1994 elections the Republicans were in control of Congress. One of the Republicans' goals was to reduce funding for AIDS in 1995 as part of a plan to cut $20 billion from the federal budget. Pelosi led the fight in the House Appropriations Committee to keep AIDS funds from being cut. She proposed that the money be taken from other projects and specified which ones she thought could receive less funding. The Appropriations Committee agreed with her by a vote of thirty-seven to eighteen. As a result, $36 million were restored for HIV prevention and for the Ryan White Care Act, which provides many different services to people with AIDS.

Because her district also has a large Chinese-American population, Pelosi concerned herself with the issue of human rights in China. In April 1989, protesters began to gather in Tiananmen Square, a large public square, in Beijing, the capital of the People's Republic of China. They were mostly young college students who were demonstrating peacefully, demanding that their government grant its people more civil rights. The student protesters were soon joined by workers, intellectuals, and civil servants. The crowds in the square increased.

By early June, the demonstrations had grown to more than 1 million people. The government felt it had to do something to stop them. On June 4th, it sent Army troops and tanks

Student flag-waver at the Tiananmen Square protests, May 1989, Tiananmen Square, Beijing. *(Courtesy of Robert Croma of London, UK, under the terms of Creative Commons License 2.0.)*

to the square to remove the demonstrators. Thousands of demonstrators were killed. People around the world were outraged at the murders. They saw the photograph published in all the major newspapers of one courageous protester standing in the square in front of four oncoming Army tanks.

Pelosi became a supporter of democracy for the people of China. She urged the U.S. government to change its trade policy toward China until it granted more freedom to its people. For three years, the U.S. waited to see if China would improve its record on human rights while it continued to grant that country most-favored-nation trade status. Such status guaranteed that China would have special advantages over other countries, such as paying lower taxes on

Pelosi meets with Chai Ling, a leader of the Chinese prodemocratic movement, in this 1990 photo. *(Courtesy of AP Images/Doug Mills)*

their products imported into the U.S. But China made no significant changes in its human rights practices.

In April 1993, Pelosi called a press conference to talk about new legislation she had co-authored with George Mitchell, a Democratic senator from Maine, that would continue China's most-favored-nation status on condition that China improve human rights for its people. The bill was called the United

States-China Act of 1993. It would provide China with $18 billion in exchange for selling its products in the United States. The U.S. thought that by keeping China's most-favored-nation status, it would encourage that country to improve its dismal record on human rights.Despite the trade benefits that come with most-favored-nation status, China continued to oppress its people. A few dissidents were released from prison, but others continued to be arrested for speaking out against the government's human rights policies and practices.

On August 23, 1987, Pelosi received the news from Baltimore that her father, Thomas D'Alesandro, Jr. had died of a heart attack. He was eighty-four years old and had lived in Baltimore's Little Italy all his life. Even as mayor of the city, he refused to move from the row house on Albermarle Street. "I'm a *paisano* (someone from the same country)," he had explained to people who asked him why he stayed there. "These are my people, and this is where I belong."

Pelosi concentrated on getting financing for the new Presidio National Park, located in San Francisco. The Presidio had been an army base since 1846. Before that, it was a Spanish out-post, and then was controlled by Mexico. The people of San Francisco wanted to preserve the Presidio because of its histori-cal importance. When the army moved most of its equipment and soldiers out of the Presidio, its more than 1,400 acres were transferred to the National Park Service and it became part of the Golden Gate National Recreation Area in 1994.

That year, Pelosi introduced a bill to keep the Presidio as part of the Golden Gate National Recreation Area. The bill passed in the House of Representatives. But, when it got to the Senate, it did not come up for a vote. The Republican-controlled Senate was busy looking for ways to cut money

Pelosi lobbied to gain funding for the Presidio National Park, seen here. *(Courtesy of AP Images/Eric Risberg)*

out of the upcoming budget, so they were not anxious to spend money on things they did not consider necessary.

With the Republicans' attempt to slash the federal budget, Pelosi and other politicians from the San Francisco area were worried that money would also be taken from the Presidio National Park. In March 1995, she introduced another bill in the House of Representatives to establish a Presidio Trust. It was a revised bill from the one she had introduced the previous year.

Pelosi's revised bill hoped to put some of the Republicans' concerns to rest. The trust would be a real estate management group composed of real estate and finance people and those who had planning backgrounds. The trust would lease out some of the park's hundreds of buildings, borrow money to improve those buildings, and make the improvements that were necessary. "This Presidio legislation anticipates the tough fiscal road ahead by taking a business-management approach to the Presidio while maintaining critical federal control and oversight," Pelosi explained. The park would be able to pay for its own upkeep and become self-sufficient in the future. As a result, funding for the park would not rely on the federal government.

On April 3, 1995, Pelosi's mother, Nancy D'Alesandro died in Baltimore at the age of eighty-six. She had been ill with heart disease and died of congestive heart failure. "She was an incredible woman who had a very major influence on me," Pelosi said about her mother. In an interview, she recalled how, when her father was in Congress, her mother "…had office hours at our home. People would come to an office in the front of our house, and she would listen to what their problems were . . . People who wanted to run for office came to her, as did people who wanted to be introduced around town . . ." She recalled that her mother had set out to become an attorney before her marriage. She attended law school, but left before she completed the coursework. "My mother was practicing public-interest law without the benefit of certification," said Pelosi. "I'll miss her terribly."

Two weeks later, Pelosi escorted two Republican congress-men around the Presidio. One representative, Ralph Regula of Ohio, was on a key House appropriations subcommittee. The other, James Hansen of Utah, was a member of the House subcommittee on national parks.

Pelosi convinced the visitors to support her bill to create the Presidio Trust. The bill passed both houses of Congress in 1996 and was signed into law by President Bill Clinton with one condition. The Presidio National Park had to be self-supporting by the year 2013.

Pelosi also served on the House Committee on Banking and Financial Services, which oversees the entire financial services industry, including the securities (stocks and bonds), insurance, banking, and housing industries.

In 1989, Pelosi introduced a provision into a bill that required the World Bank and other development banks to review the impact on the environment of the projects they finance and to make their findings available to the public. The bill was signed into law as the International Development and Finance Act of 1989.

The provision that Pelosi added to the bill became known as the "Pelosi amendment." It requires banks to turn down any project that has not had an environmental impact assessment or any project whose environmental impact assessment has not been available to the public for 120 days.

Pelosi was also a member of the U. S. House Permanent Select Committee on Intelligence (known as the House Intelligence Committee). This committee votes to authorize appropriations for the intelligence and intelligence-related activities of the U.S. government, including the Central Intelligence Agency, the National Security Agency, and the intelligence activities of the Department of Defense, Department of the Army, the Department of the Navy, and the Department of the Air Force.

She also served on the Committee on Standards of Official Conduct (known as the Ethics Committee) for six years. This group determines what is proper behavior for members of the House with respect to things like accepting gifts, travel, and campaign financing. It also investigates inappropriate behavior of its members and suggests to the House proper punishment for those members who have not conducted themselves properly. When House Speaker Newt Gingrich was investigated for having used funds from a political action committee (PAC) to pay for a televised "town meeting" and for a college course that he taught, Pelosi was one of four members of the Investigative Subcommittee who looked into his conduct. She also served as a member of a bipartisan (Democrats and Republicans) task force whose job it was to update the rules and procedures of the committee.

In 1998, President Bill Clinton announced that he planned to visit the People's Republic of China, where he would be formally received in Tiananmen Square. That June, Pelosi voted in favor of a resolution asking President Clinton to reconsider his decision to visit China until that country acknowledged that they had massacred student protesters in 1989, promised to improve its record on human rights, and released the Chinese students who were still in jail ten years later. It was a non-binding resolution that was little more than a suggestion to the president. The resolution passed in the House, but not in the Senate, and was never presented to the president.

In 1999, Pelosi announced that she planned to run for the office of House Majority Whip in the next term. She created a political action committee called "PAC to the Future," to help raise money for Democrats running for Congress in the 2000 elections. She raised $3 million in the hope that the Democrats would win enough seats to take over control of the House from the Republicans. If the Democrats won control, the office of House Majority Whip would become the third-highest position in the Democratic Party.

The Democrats did not achieve their goal of becoming the majority party in the House. After the elections of 2000, Republicans were still in control, but Pelosi's hard work to raise money for Democratic candidates was greatly appreciated. Her goal of becoming one of the highest-ranking women in Congress took a great leap forward. "She is truly a star in her work on behalf of the Democratic Party. She has raised more money for more candidates than any other member outside the leadership," Representative Patrick Kennedy of Rhode Island said. Kennedy was the chairman of the Democratic Congressional Campaign Committee and was in charge of the party's effort to win back the House.

Pelosi continued her efforts to improve health care. Along with Senator John Kerry of Massachusetts, she co-sponsored the Vaccines for a New Millennium Act in 2000 to provide tax incentives to biotechnology and drug manufacturing companies to accelerate the development of vaccines against deadly infectious diseases. "Every year, TB (tuberculosis), malaria and HIV/AIDS kill over seven million people," she said. "Vaccines are our best hope to bring these and other epidemics under control. But accelerated research efforts are needed if we are to develop these vaccines in the near future." She was also instrumental in bringing the Microbicide Development Act of 2000 to the floor of the House. This legislation would increase funding for research and development in new methods of preventing the spread of disease.

five

House Minority Whip

When Representative David Bonior of Michigan announced in 2001 that he would not continue on as House Minority Whip, Nancy Pelosi was an eight-term member of the House of Representatives. She had been reelected every two years after her first win in 1988. She decided to run for the position of Minority Whip. Representative Steny Hoyer of Maryland wanted the position as well.

The position of whip is the second most powerful leadership position in the House of Representatives. When a political party is in control—the majority party—the position is called the House Majority Whip. When they are not in control, as the Democrats were not in 2001, the position is known as the House Minority Whip.

The term "whip" has its origin in the British fox hunts. In order to make certain that the dogs chasing the fox during a hunt did not wander away, but remained with the pack,

a "whipper-in",
who carried a
whip, rode with
the hunters. It
was the whipper-
in's job to crack
the whip to make
the straying dogs
return to the pack.
Legislatures in
Britain and
in other coun-
tries adopted the
idea of a whip
for their mem-
bers who enforce
party discipline
and make certain
that those mem-
bers are present
when important
votes are taken.

Steny Hoyer

In the United States, the whip is in charge of keeping track of the schedule for the House of Representatives on a daily basis. When issues are being discussed on the floor, the whip sees to it that the rules and procedures that the members follow are fair to everyone. The whip must make sure that members with differing opinions on the issues are heard. Other duties of the whip include assisting party leaders with their tasks, distributing information to party members, and tracking important legislation.

The whip must be a disciplinarian, who makes certain that party members vote the way the leadership prefers on bills that come before them. The whip must also be able to gently persuade members that a yes or no vote is the proper one. David Bonior felt that Pelosi had both of those qualities and he endorsed her for the position. Representative John Murtha of Pennsylvania managed her campaign.

Both Pelosi and Hoyer claimed to have enough votes to win. Pelosi said that electing a woman as whip would "promote diversity in the caucus ." Hoyer maintained that the 120 votes Pelosi expected to be in her favor were not assured. He expected that a broader range of Democrats—liberal, moderate, conservative—would vote for him. He accused Pelosi of being too liberal to appeal to moderate and conservative Democrats. Pelosi told him, "The idea of right-left, moderate-conservative-liberal doesn't mean very much."

Her assessment turned out to be correct. A secret vote was held among the members of the House to elect the new Minority Whip. Pelosi defeated Steny Hoyer by a vote of 118 to ninety-five. On January 15, 2002, a historical transfer of leadership took place. Nancy Pelosi took over the position of House Minority Whip, the first woman in history to rise to that position. She also became the highest-ranking woman ever elected to an office in the federal government.

On February 5th, Pelosi was formally sworn in as House Minority Whip. A number of members of the House indicated that they wanted to officially congratulate her on her promotion and to welcome her as Minority Whip. W. Douglas Smith of South Carolina was the Speaker pro tempore who presided over the House on that day. The Speaker pro tempore is the temporary speaker who conducts the business of the House

David Bonior congratulates Pelosi by presenting her with a whip after her successful bid to gain the position of House Minority Whip. *(Courtesy of AP Images/Joe Marquette)*

when the Speaker is absent. On February 5th, Smith called on the members who wanted to speak and granted each one five minutes to make their welcoming speech. Several members who spoke were from California and had worked with Pelosi before and after she was first elected to Congress."Mr. Speaker, I join my colleagues today in celebration of the official swearing-in of the Democratic whip, my colleague and friend, Nancy Pelosi . . . ," said Lucille Roybal-Allard. "Nancy was a leader in California and in the California Democratic party for many years before her election to Congress in 1987. In many ways, her political experience provided a model for me in becoming the first Mexican-American woman to be elected to Congress, and I have appreciated the many ways she has supported me both before and after I joined her here in the House in 1993." The Speaker pro tempore also called on Barbara Lee, who said, "Mr. Speaker, as we celebrate and honor our new minority whip, the gentlewoman from California, I also must really thank her for being such a role model. As a wife, a mother, a grandmother, a friend to many, a great humanitarian and a phenomenal leader, Ms. Pelosi has really demonstrated that women can do it all at the same time." She went on to say, "Nancy, congratulations on earning this place in history. Congratulations and Godspeed as you

Barbara Lee, Pelosi's fellow representative from California, congratulated Pelosi with a welcoming speech after Pelosi was elected House Minority Whip. *(Courtesy of AP Images/Mike Fiala)*

After the terrorist attacks of 9/11, Pelosi approved of President Bush's plan to find and capture terrorist leader Osama bin Laden, but she did not agree with his decision to invade Iraq. *(Courtesy of FEMA)*

accept this place of distinction in the people's House. I know that there are many girls and young women throughout the world who are saying, 'When I grow up, I want to be just like Congresswoman Pelosi.'"

In 2001, Pelosi became the top-ranking Democrat on the House Permanent Select Committee on Intelligence. When terrorists flew airplanes into New York's World Trade Center, Washington D.C.'s Pentagon, and a field in Pennsylvania,

Pelosi approved of President George Bush's decision to find the terrorist leader Osama bin Laden and bring him to justice. Bin Laden was the leader of the terrorist group called al Qaeda. Nineteen of their members piloted the airplanes. Soon after the attack, Pelosi said, "We must assist New York in its recovery effort. As a person from earthquake country [California experiences many earthquakes], I know what it means to a people when they know that the federal government is there with you in time of disaster. So I think we have to remove all doubt in the minds of anybody in New York or elsewhere that the federal government will be there for New York. It's not only in New York's interest, it's in our country's interest." A month later, the U.S. retaliated by bombing selected military targets in Afghanistan, the country from which the September 11th terrorists came. The bombings were followed by sending in ground troops in an attempt to find Osama bin Laden.

Thirteen months after the invasion of Afghanistan, President Bush told the American people that it was time to invade Iraq, an Arab nation in the Middle East. The president and others in his administration said that Iraq's dictator, Saddam Husscin, had chcmical, biological, and nuclcar wcapons that threatened the security of the U.S.

Pelosi spoke out against the invasion, saying that the president should concentrate instead on al Qaeda and the war on terror. "Can we conclude that the threat is best eliminated by going to war now?" she asked the President at a meeting in the Cabinet Room of the White House on February 5, 2002. "Any fissile (nuclear) material Saddam Hussein gets is from the outside. It's a global problem, and we don't have a global solution." She favored trying to find a diplomatic solution rather than going to war against Hussein. Her reasons included the cost on the American economy, concerns that an Iraq invasion would deflect attention and resources from the war against terror, and the loss of American lives. "We must protect our men and women in uniform," she said, speaking to the members of the House of Representatives as they debated a resolution to go to war against Saddam Hussein. "They are courageous. They risk their lives for our freedom, for our country. We cannot put them in harm's way unless we take every measure possible to protect them . . . If we go in, certainly we can show our power to Saddam Hussein. If we resolve this issue diplomatically, we can show our strength as a great country . . . Let us show our greatness. Vote no on this resolution." In October 2002, the resolution came up for a vote in the House of Representatives. Although 126 Democrats and one hundred Republicans voted against the invasion of Iraq, it passed by a vote of 296-133. In the Senate, the vote was 77-23 in favor of invading Iraq if Saddam Hussein did not give up his weapons of mass destruction.

Pelosi had become the highest-ranking Democrat on the House Permanent Select Committee on Intelligence. She voted against the resolution. "I have seen no evidence or intelligence that suggests that Iraq indeed poses an imminent threat to our nation," she said. "If the [Bush] Administration has that information, they have not shared it with the Congress."

President Bush was commander-in-chief of the armed forces and had the final word on sending troops into battle. On March 20, 2003, U.S. forces invaded Iraq. The purpose of the invasion, said Bush, was to get rid of the weapons of mass destruction, to remove Hussein from office, and to free the Iraqi people from his tyranny.

Campaign finance reform also became an important issue in late 2001. The American people believed that special interest groups—certain industries, corporations, and individuals—had too much influence over Congress because they contributed large amounts of money to the election campaigns of individual members. They wanted Congress to reform, or fix, the campaign finance law, so that Congress could not use contributions from special interest groups to influence the political campaigns of individual representatives and senators.

Congressmen Christopher Shays of Connecticut and Martin Meehan of Massachusetts introduced their campaign finance reform resolution, called the Shays-Meehan bill, in the House on June 28, 2001.

Pelosi's job as whip was to get enough votes from Democratic members of the House to pass the bill. She saw to it that all members of the House were present when the bill came up for a vote. The bill easily passed in the House on February 14, 2002 and went on to the Senate. In the meantime, the Senate had introduced its own bill on campaign finance reform. Called the McCain-Feingold bill in honor of its co-sponsors, John McCain of Arizona and Russ Feingold of Wisconsin, it was similar in many respects to the House version. The Senate passed its version of the campaign finance reform bill.

In an interview, Pelosi was asked whether she thought the president would sign the bill. "I think the president will sign the bill," she answered. "It had strong bipartisan support [support from both the Democrats and the Republicans in Congress] . . . the bill passed because the American people wanted it to pass. And as Congress heard their voices, so, too, will the president." She agreed that campaign reform would certainly change how money contributed by special interest groups influence Congress. But, she thought that it would "do nothing to hurt the ability of parties to reach out, register voters, get them to the polls, educate them about the issues."

She recalled how candidates running for office respected campaign finance law when she had chaired the Democratic Party in California during the 1970s. But that had changed in recent years. "The law . . . says that federal candidates are not supposed to be raising corporate money. And somehow or other, in the last decade or two, there has been this addiction that has occurred to large contributions for a federal purpose that is counter to the spirit of the law." For that reason, she thought it necessary to reform the law.

A bipartisan bill, the result of debate on both the House and Senate campaign finance reform bills was finally agreed upon and was sent to the president for his signature. President Bush signed it into law on March 27, 2002.

By 2002, Pelosi had become the highest-ranking member of the House Committee on Appropriations, serving on its Foreign Operations Subcommittee. She was a member of its Labor, Health, Human Services, and Education Subcommittee as well.

Pelosi's commitment to increased funding for HIV and AIDS research continued. She became the co-chair of the House Democratic Caucus' AIDS Task Force and also campaigned actively for increased funding for breast cancer research and prevention.

Pelosi had worked for years on environmental issues, such as the protection of the Arctic National Wildlife Refuge in

Pelosi gained support from environmentalists for her stand on environmental issues, such as her vote to protect the Arctic National Wildlife Refuge in Alaska, seen here. *(Courtesy of AP Images/Arctic National Wildlife Refuge)*

Alaska and the red rock canyons of Utah. She also worked tirelessly on the issue of reducing logging in the national forests of the U.S. For the next year, Pelosi continued to work on the issues that were important to her, to the Democrats, and to the country. In 2002, leadership changes in Congress again led to her making another historical decision.

six
House Minority Leader

I n November 2002, Nancy Pelosi again made history when she became the first woman ever elected House Minority Leader. For the first time in U.S. history, a woman would lead a political party in Congress.

She had just won reelection in her home district and had raised money for Democrats across the country. She was well-known nationally by Democrats by this time, both for her role as minority whip and for the funds her political action committee distributed to diverse candidates. She also traveled to many states to help raise money for local Democratic candidates.

The Democrats failed to win control of the House of Representatives in the November 2002 elections. When Representative Richard Gephardt of Missouri, who had been House minority leader, announced he intended to give up the position, Pelosi decided to run for it. She had started lining up commitments from members of the Democratic caucus that they would vote for her even before the elections and Gephardt's announcement. "Politics is about motion," she said. "You are either going forward, or you are going backward." And forward was the direction Nancy Pelosi wanted to go.

Representative Martin Frost of Texas wanted to be House Minority Leader as well. Both he and Pelosi campaigned hard for the position. Both candidates had taken similar positions in their voting records. Pelosi's votes were consistently aligned with the positions held by labor, environmental, and consumer groups. Frost's votes, too, showed that he favored organized labor.

However, there were some differences. Pelosi had voted against the war in Iraq, but Frost had supported it. Pelosi

Martin Frost *(Courtesy of AP Photo/Harry Cabluck)*

had always been opposed to trade with China based on its dismal human rights record. Frost had voted to normalize trade relations with that country.

While Pelosi was seen as a liberal Democrat, some conservative members of the House respected her abilities as a fundraiser and as a speaker for Democratic candidates. Frost was more conservative, but he had some liberal support as well. However, it was expected from the start of the race that Pelosi would win. If she became the new House minority leader, Pelosi's position was very clear. She wanted the Democrats to work toward winning back control of the House of Representatives. She felt that the Democrats should challenge the administration of President George W. Bush and the Republicans aggressively. To do that, the Democrats would need to have a very clear message about how they would govern the country differently. They had to define their positions on both domestic and international issues. Frost's position on winning control of Congress was less focused. He also spent time attacking Pelosi. He hoped to get members of the voting caucus who were committed to Pelosi to change their minds and vote for him instead. His strategy didn't work. Just before the election, it became clear to Frost that Pelosi had more votes promised to her by the members of the caucus than he did. He dropped out of the race and supported Pelosi's candidacy instead, promising to work with her to bring control of the House of Representatives back to the Democrats. With Frost's withdrawal, Representative Harold Ford of Tennessee decided to challenge Pelosi for the position as House minority leader. He thought he could work better with the Republicans than Pelosi could. But Pelosi was confident that she would have enough votes to beat Ford.

During the campaign, Pelosi talked about her experience and abilities. "I didn't run as a woman," she said later. "I presented my credentials as an experienced legislator, skilled organizer, astute (smart) politician. I didn't want anyone to vote for me or against me because I was a woman. But the fact that I am a woman is a giant bonus."

In her first run for office in 1987, she had defended herself against opponents who claimed her wealth put her out of touch with her constituents. Now she had to defend herself against opponents who said her liberal voting record put her out of touch with the Republican-controlled, conservative Congress. Pelosi promised to work with Congress toward achieving goals that she believed to be in the national interest. "Where we [Democrats and Republicans] can find our common ground, we shall seek it. Where we cannot find that common ground, we must stand our ground," she added.

The vote was held on November 14th. Pelosi won by a 177-29 margin. It was expected that liberal Democrats would vote for her, but it turned out that moderates and conservatives voted for her as well.

Her primary job as House minority leader was to help Democratic candidates win election and reelection to the House. Pelosi argued that Democrats must distinguish themselves from Republicans. She knew that they would have to be unified and their vision for the future of America had to be distinct from the Republican vision.

As House minority leader, Pelosi had to deal with people and the problems they considered urgent. Pelosi told an interviewer that raising a family prepared her to do that. "When you raise five children born six years apart, you do most of the work yourself. You can't attract a good deal of people to

Pelosi celebrates with Richard Gephardt after being the first woman elected to serve as House Minority Leader. *(Courtesy of AP Images/Ken Lambert)*

help out. It trains you to anticipate, to be organized and to be flexible," she said.

She announced soon after her election as House Minority Leader that she would focus her energies on the issues of national security, the environment, and the economy.

On the issue of national security, Pelosi said that much work still needed to be done, as the U.S. saw when the World Trade Center in New York and the Pentagon in Washington, D.C. were attacked on September 11, 2001. It was obvious to Pelosi that the U.S. couldn't deal with eliminating terrorism on its own. It required the efforts of all civilized nations working together to do that.

About the economy, she said that the difference between the Republicans' plan for tax cuts and the Democrats' plan to stimulate the economy and help it grow was very clear. The Democratic Party believed in stimulating the economy in a financially responsible way. On the other hand, the Republicans wanted to offer huge tax cuts to wealthy individuals and corporations, which Pelosi believed would not stimulate the economy.

A month after her election as House minority leader, Pelosi spoke about how the Democratic plan would stimulate the economy to grow. "Our plans, just our stimulus package, will create one million new jobs. The president has lost 1.7 million jobs in his first two years of office. And by the White House's own calculations, he will only create 170,000 jobs with his plan."

She voted against the Republican tax-cut bills in 2003, as she had in 2001. She thought that the U. S. could not afford more tax cuts. She argued that the Republican tax cuts would benefit the wealthy segment of American society and would do nothing to help the working people of America. Instead of reducing the national deficit, the proposed tax cuts would contribute to increasing it.

In June 2003, Pelosi received an award from a California environmental group for her continuing efforts to get environmental legislation passed in the House. When she received the award, she called the environment a civil right. "Our children deserve a safe and healthy environment. Every child has a right to clean air to breath! Every child has a right to clean water to drink! And every child—especially poor children

Pelosi has called President Bush "an incompetent leader," and has been vocal in her disagreement with the Bush administration's policies and agendas. *(Courtesy of AP Images/Evan Vucci)*

who live near health hazards—has a right to be born into an environment free of deadly pollutants and toxic waste!" She promised to continue her efforts for children and the environment as House Minority Leader. Then she hammered President Bush and the Republicans. "Sadly, others have a different priority," she said. "Quickly and quietly in the

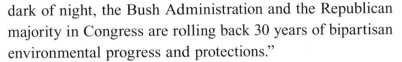

dark of night, the Bush Administration and the Republican majority in Congress are rolling back 30 years of bipartisan environmental progress and protections."

Pelosi set out to achieve one more goal as House minority leader. She wanted to be a role model for young women. "People try to instill doubt a woman can do a certain job when she's 'the first,' whether it's the first woman to head a major corporation or the first woman Army general," she said. "I consider this a challenge to remove all doubt in anyone's mind that women can do any job in America." She wanted the effects of her being 'the first' woman elected as House minority leader felt even after she left office.

In 2004, Pelosi spoke out again on the Iraq war and President Bush's handling of it. In an interview on the TV program, *Meet the Press*, she said, "we're on a course of action that is dangerous to our troops. We did not equip them well. A Department of Defense report said that a quarter of the troops would not have lost their lives or been injured if they were better equipped. This is just absolutely an unacceptable situation. And for over a year, it has existed."

By this time, Saddam Hussein had been taken prisoner and no weapons of mass destruction had been found in Iraq. The invasion of Iraq should have been over, but instead the war escalated when insurgents and others began attacking U.S. troops. Before long, sections of the country suffered daily bombings and other attacks. The Bush administration war planners had not counted on that happening.

Pelosi had said earlier that she thought George Bush was not fit for the position of president. "Bush is an incompetent leader," she said. "In fact, he's not a leader . . . He's a person who has no judgment, no experience and no knowledge of the subjects that he has to decide upon . . . He has on his shoulders the deaths of many more troops."

When she was reminded of that statement later, she replied that she had said that with great reluctance and after many requests about what his administration's plans were for Iraq. She said she had also visited the troops in Iraq and Afghanistan, in the German hospitals where wounded troops were sent, and in U.S. hospitals.

She saw firsthand what the soldiers faced on the battle field and felt "We owe them at least a fair fight when they go into battle for us. And that means they have to have leadership that knows what's on the ground when they get there, the equipment to make the fight, the intelligence to know who the adversary is." She felt that the commander-in-chief [President Bush] was responsible for providing proper and up-to-date intelligence and that he had not done that.

Late in 2002, the National Commission on Terrorist Attacks Upon the United States, also known as the September 11th Commission, was created to investigate the circumstances surrounding the attacks of September 11, 2001. It was asked to provide recommendations that would protect the U. S. against future attacks. The commission was a ten-member bipartisan group headed by Thomas Kean, a former governor of New Jersey and Lee Hamilton, a former congressman from Indiana.

On July 22, 2004, the September 11th Commission reported on its findings and recommended ways in which America's intelligence operations should be changed to improve the country's security. Among its recommendations was the creation of a position of national intelligence director. President Bush immediately nominated the chairman of the House

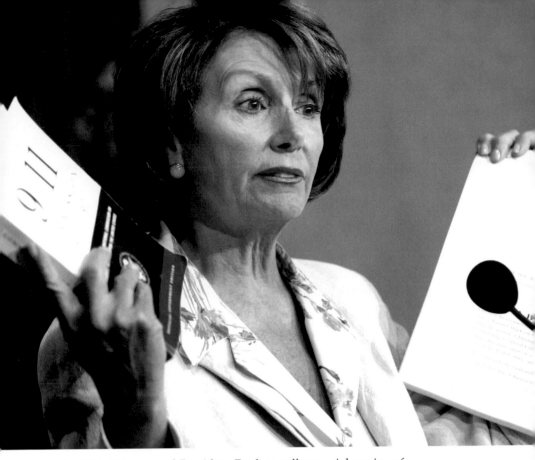

In 2004, Pelosi urged President Bush to call a special session of Congress to address the September 11th Commission's findings. In this photo, Pelosi displays a copy of the 9/11 Commission Report. *(Courtesy of AP Images/Lawrence Jackson)*

Intelligence Committee, Porter Goss of Florida, as the new director for national intelligence.

Congress had already recessed for six weeks that summer as it did every year. Its members were not expected to return to Washington until after Labor Day. Pelosi urged President Bush to call a special session of Congress to pass the September 11th Commission's recommendations into law immediately. New York and Washington were on an elevated terrorism alert at the time. There was also concern that the terrorists would launch another attack just before the presidential election in November.

Pelosi felt it was urgent for Congress to vote on the recommendations as soon as possible. She said, "The question should be asked of Republicans: How can you take a six-week vacation from Congress?" and promised the American people, "We will not allow this report to gather dust or to be shredded."

She was concerned that waiting until Congress returned to Washington in the fall would not leave enough time to pass legislation on the recommendations. Both the House and the Senate would have to hold hearings and discussions before they voted on the recommendations. But, despite Pelosi's concerns, there was little action in Congress to implement them.

But Pelosi was able to fulfill one promise she had made to the Democrats. By September 2004, she and the other members of her caucus brought forth a six-point plan that they called the "New Partnership for America's Future." Pelosi said the plan showed how committed House Democrats were to building a strong middle class, as well as providing for national security, prosperity and opportunity for all citizens. They would also deal with members of Congress, making certain that they behaved properly and honorably, and to make those who did not accountable for their behavior. The Democrats hoped that the plan would assure that they win control of the House of Representatives from the Republicans in the 2004 elections. But, that did not happen. When the votes were counted, the Republicans were still in control of both the House and the Senate.

By 2006, the administration of President George Bush had become increasingly unpopular with the American people. An Associated Press-Ipsos poll showed that two thirds of

In May of 2006, Pelosi once again pushed for the Democratic Party to take control of the House. *(Courtesy of AP Images/Joe Marquette)*

the country felt that the president was not doing a good job. They thought that the Republicans in Congress were performing poorly in their jobs as well. In May, Pelosi promised that, should the Democrats take control of the House in the November elections, they would begin to investigate these issues and make changes to benefit the American people.

seven

The Midterm Elections of 2006

The American people had become dissatisfied with the Republican administration and with George Bush's conduct of the war in Iraq. They were also unhappy with the high price of gasoline, scandals involving officials in government, and the administration's poor response to Hurricane Katrina.

Hurricane Katrina was one of the deadliest storms to hit the southeastern coast of the United States. It came onshore on August 29, 2005, and devastated the coastal parts of Alabama, Georgia, Florida, and especially, Louisiana. A levee in New Orleans, Louisiana, had broken and tons of water rushed in and flooded eighty percent of that city.

On March 2, 2006, Nancy Pelosi and a thirty-five member congressional delegation arrived in New Orleans to see for themselves the damage that Hurricane Katrina had caused and how the restoration work was going. They saw rubble

Pelosi talks with Sister Mary Rose in the French Quarter of New Orleans while participating in a congressional tour of the areas heavily affected by Hurricane Katrina. *(Courtesy of AP Images/Alex Brandon)*

everywhere; survivors were still without food, water, and shelter six months after the hurricane hit.

It was obvious that the agencies of the federal government—especially FEMA (Federal Emergency Management Agency)—had been slow to help people who needed it. "I'm not absolutely certain that our federal agencies on the ground here are meeting that challenge," Pelosi said.

Many Republicans in Congress had also become less enthusiastic about backing the president's policies. Those who were running for election or reelection in 2006 were afraid they would lose if they did. The Democrats saw this as the best opportunity to win additional seats in Congress and take control of both the House of Representatives and the Senate.

In the House, the Democrats needed to win fifteen additional seats to achieve their goal. If they did, it was almost certain that Nancy Pelosi would be elected Speaker of the House, one of the most important positions in the U.S. government. The Speaker of the House is second in line to become president of the United States if the president dies or for another reason cannot continue in office. If Nancy Pelosi became Speaker of the House, it would be the first time in the history of the United States that a woman served in that position.

Pelosi made certain that her caucus of Democratic leaders were united in opposition to the policies of the Bush administration. She was a disciplinarian who saw to it that all Democrats voted the way caucus members wanted them to on bills that came before the House. She raised more money for the Democrats than any other fundraiser. She campaigned for Democratic candidates in many parts of the country. In the three months preceding the elections, Pelosi traveled to nearly two dozen states to help Democrats running for office.

She was determined to do everything she could to assure Democratic wins. In December 2005, Pelosi had spoken to reporters during her weekly news conference in her office. She had told them, "I fully intend to be standing here as Speaker of the House next year . . ."

In the spring of 2006, tensions increased between the United States and the People's Republic of China. There was a trade deficit between the two countries in which the United States imported six times more goods from China than it exported.

Part of the reason for that was because China's money was cheaper and, therefore, its products cost less when paid for with U.S. dollars. U.S. manufacturers, looking to save money, were buying goods from China rather than having them made at a higher price in the United States.

U.S. trade practices with China had been problematic for Pelosi for many years. She still wanted to see a change in China's status as a most-favored-nation where trade was concerned. In March, she said, "Members of Congress, on a bipartisan basis, are expressing serious concerns that China's national currency is undervalued and causing harm to the U.S. economy and sending American jobs overseas."

Confident that they had a good chance of winning control of the House, Pelosi and the Democratic leaders planned their course of action in the months and weeks before the elections. "We have to be ready to win, and we have to tell [voters] what we will do when we win," Pelosi said in an interview early in May 2006. The Democrats wanted to raise the minimum wage, change parts of the prescription drug law, put new homeland security measures into effect, and control the budget deficit that the Republicans had caused.

Pelosi also promised that the House would begin an investigation into some of the Bush administration's activities, including the intelligence reports that said Saddam Hussein had weapons of mass destruction. This inaccurate intelligence led to the invasion of Iraq. They would look into how widespread the administration's wiretapping of Americans suspected of having telephone conversations with terrorists was. They would also investigate the billions of government dollars wasted in Iraq and Afghanistan by private companies working there. "You never know where it leads to," she said about the future investigations.

By August 2006, leading congressional Democrats were calling for President Bush to begin to withdraw American troops from Iraq and to complete the withdrawal by the end of 2006. It was clear that the war in Iraq would be the major issue in the midterm elections that year.

Under Pelosi's leadership, the Democrats prepared their agenda for the 2006 elections. They promised honest leadership and an open government. They wanted to make the United States energy independent, reducing America's dependence on foreign oil. Democrats would also eliminate the billions of dollars in subsidies that oil and gas companies received and put the money into the search for alternative sources of energy.

The Democratic agenda included a health care system so the U.S. would join other industrialized nations in assuring that everyone would have access to affordable health care. The Democrats wanted to fix the government's prescription drug program for senior citizens, called Medicare Part D, so that older people would be able to afford their medication. They would also invest money in stem cell research and other medical research that would help prevent and cure various illnesses and diseases. Research involving stem cells uses human embryos (the earliest stage in the process of creating a baby) to grow many different kinds of cells in the laboratory. President Bush was not in favor of stem cell research or of using federal money to fund the research.

Providing security for the United States was also important. In their agenda, that would include protecting Americans both at home and abroad, provide a strong national defense,

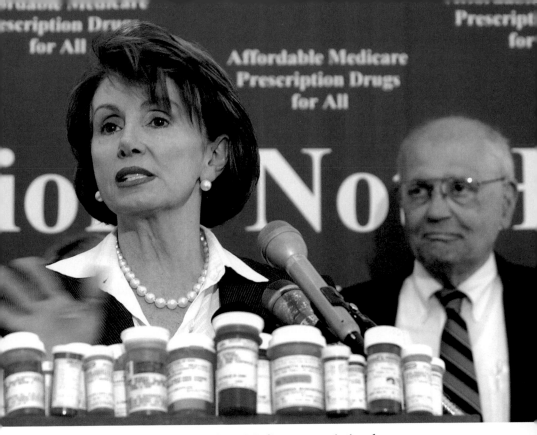

In this photo, Pelosi speaks about Medicare prescription drug legislation. Fixing the government's prescription drug program for senior citizens was part of the Democratic Party's agenda during 2006. *(Courtesy of AP Images/Dennis Cook)*

and honor the sacrifices made by the troops by taking care of them when they came home and by caring for their families as well. Pelosi argued that the Bush administration had not done enough to assure the security of Americans. "In these times of unprecedented challenge and change, real leadership demands preparing for the threats that exist today and those that will emerge tomorrow," she said. "It demands tough and smart policies that recognize that a stronger America begins at home." The Democratic agenda would address the issue of security for the U.S.

Another issue the Democrats considered important was economic prosperity and educational excellence. They wanted to raise the minimum wage, make college tuition tax-deductible, and reduce the huge budget deficit the Republicans had caused by spending less federal money in the future.

Finally, they wanted all Americans to have security when they retire. The Democratic agenda would include changing the pension system, expanding savings incentives to encourage people to save more of their money, and preventing the Social Security Administration from being made private instead of having it continue to be run by the government, something President Bush talked about doing.

In the midterm elections, held on November 7, 2006, voters elected local politicians, including the men and women who would represent them in the House of Representatives for two years. They would also vote on those senators who were up for reelection. Senators are elected for a six-year tem; a third of the senate is up for reelection every two years.

In San Francisco, Pelosi was up for reelection in her home district. She ran against Michael DeNunzio, chairman of the San Francisco Republican Party, who had little chance of winning. Pelosi won reelection handily.

The Democrats also won around most of the country. When the votes were counted Democrats and independents (those not affiliated with any political party) who would vote with them had won thirty new seats. The Democrats were the majority party. The Senate was evenly divided—fifty Democrats and fifty Republicans, including Vice President Dick Cheney, a Republican, who presides over the Senate and votes on bills in case of a tie. It took another day for the votes to be counted in the race for Senate in Virginia. But, after they were, the Democrats hade fifty-one members in

Pelosi celebrates as the Democratic Party gains the majority in both the House and the Senate during the 2006 midterm elections. *(Courtesy of AP Images/J. Scott Applewhite)*

the Senate and would be the majority party there as well as in the House.

"It was a thumpin'," President Bush admitted when the final election results were in. "It's clear the Democrat (sic) Party had a good night." Bush went on to promise to work with the new Democratic leadership and invited its members to lunch in the Oval Office of the White House.

Nancy Pelosi was among those who attended the lunch. Afterwards, she said, "I met with President Bush at the White House two days after the election, and we both extended

Pelosi shakes hands with President Bush in the Oval Office following the Democratic victories of the 2006 elections. *(Courtesy of AP Images/Pablo Martinez Monsivais)*

the hand of friendship. We recognized that we have our differences, and we will debate them as our Founding Fathers intended, but we will do so in a way that gets results for the American people."

The Democrats clearly had their work cut out for them. On the day after the elections, Pelosi told reporters that the American people wanted their elected officials to lead them in a new direction. "But nowhere was the call for new direction more clear from the American people than in the war in Iraq. This is something that we must work on together with the president. We know that 'stay the course' is not working," she said, referring to President Bush's assertion that America and its allies were winning the war in Iraq and should continue to do that they have done for the past three years.

Secretary of Defense Donald Rumsfeld had been in charge of the war since the invasion in the spring of 2003. As the situation in Iraq worsened there had been several calls in Congress and elsewhere for Rumsfeld to be fired. But President Bush refused to fire his defense secretary. Then, on the day after the elections, Rumsfeld resigned as secretary of defense and the president accepted his resignation.

Pelosi commented on the change in leadership at the Department of Defense. "The president's acceptance of Defense Secretary Donald Rumsfeld's resignation on Wednesday is an encouraging step, an opportunity for a fresh start in Iraq, and I hope a precursor to a change in policy."

She also promised other changes, including a more open and more honest government. "We certainly have a mandate for making this place [Washington, D.C.] more honest, making it operate in a more civilized way. Democrats intend to lead the most honest, the most open and the most ethical Congress in history."

But the House of Representatives still had one very important election to go through before they could begin to work for the changes the American people wanted. They had to elect their leader, the Speaker of the House.

eight
A New Direction for America

After the 2006 elections the Democrats were the majority party in both houses of Congress. By November 9th, it was apparent that the Democrats would elect Nancy Pelosi Speaker of the House. As Speaker, she would have three important roles to play. She still represented her district in San Francisco and would continue to serve her constituents there. In addition, the Speaker is the head of her party as well as the leader of the House. But, the most important job of the Speaker is to preside over the House of Representatives.

The Speaker calls the House to order when it is in session and administers the oath of office to new members. The Speaker decides which issues and bills will be debated and voted upon and in what order. She calls on members in turn to speak on the House floor and maintains order. The Speaker is also in charge of the committees and subcommittees that help decide what the final bills contain before they are voted upon.

The House of Representatives voted for its speaker on November 16, 2006. One by one, the outgoing Speaker, J. Dennis Hastert of Illinois, a Republican, called on the members. Each member called out his or her choice. Republicans voted for Representative John Boehner of Ohio, the House Republican leader, but Pelosi was elected Speaker of the House by a margin of 233 to 202. The vote was along party lines.

On January 4, 2007, the House was called into session for its new term. As was the tradition, the name of each of the 435 members was called by the clerk of the House. Each member announced his or her choice for speaker. After the votes were tallied and it was determined that Nancy Pelosi would be the next speaker, John Boehner told the House, "In a few moments, I'll have the high privilege of handing the gavel of the House of Representatives to a woman for the first time in American history. Whether you are a Democrat, Republican or independent, today is a cause for celebration."

Nancy Pelosi was sworn in as Speaker of the House by Representative John Dingell of Michigan, an honor awarded him for serving in the House longer than any of the other representatives. Then Boehner handed her the gavel, which she would use to call the House to order in the future.

"I accept this gavel in the spirit of partnership, not partisanship, and I look forward to working with you, Mr. Boehner, and the Republicans in the Congress for the good of the American people," said Pelosi.

The floor of the House was filled with both new and returning members. The new speaker's family and friends joined relatives of other members, filling the upstairs gallery. Paul Pelosi, the five Pelosi children, plus their spouses and their own children had come to witness this historical

Pelosi banging the gavel as Speaker of the House *(Courtesy of AP Images/ Susan Walsh)*

event. Pelosi's brother Tommy, and John Burton, the former California representative and Nancy Pelosi's mentor, were there too.

In the tradition of opening day, family members included the children and grandchildren of House members. Pelosi's six grandchildren, including her latest, a two-month old grandson,

After being elected Speaker of the House, Pelosi invited her grandchildren to touch the gavel. *(Courtesy of AP Images/Pablo Martinez Monsivais)*

attended their grandmother's swearing-in ceremony. Pelosi invited the children up to the rostrum to touch the speaker's gavel. Then, pounding the speaker's gavel on the rostrum, she called the House to order.

As soon as she was sworn in, Pelosi swore in the other members. She then promised to work with the Republicans, but she also bluntly warned President Bush that the Democrats would oppose any attempt to increase the number of American troops in Iraq. "The American people rejected an open-ended obligation to a war without end," she told him to a standing ovation by the Democrats.

She went on to explain, "It is the responsibility of the president to articulate a new plan for Iraq that makes it clear to the Iraqis that they must defend their own streets and their own security, a plan that promotes stability in the region and a plan that allows us to responsibly redeploy our troops."

However, as commander-in-chief of the armed forces, the president has the final say about deploying troops anywhere in the world. All Congress can do is to refuse to appropriate money to pay for the deployment. President Bush insisted that he would send additional troops to Iraq and that the war there could be won.

The House got to work on drafting legislation that would address the issues that the American people said, through their votes, were important to them. The Democrats called it "a new direction for America" and promised to try to fulfill their election promises set forth in their agenda.

The Democrats in the House wanted to complete their work within the first hundred working hours of being called into session. Pelosi promised that they would address issues that included making America secure, jobs, health care, energy independence, and education. Under her leadership, the House started drafting legislation on those issues.

On January 9, they passed the first of the six bills. This one would enact many of the recommendations from the September 11 Commission. The commission had looked into the terrorist attacks on the United States and studied America's response to it and its plans for keeping America safe from further terrorist attacks. The House bill would make it mandatory within three to five years for all air cargo and ship containers coming to the United States to be screened for explosives and other terrorist devices.

The following day, the House passed a new minimum wage bill that would raise the minimum wage from the present $5.15

Pelosi and other members of Congress applaud during a press conference held to discuss Democratic legislation passed during the first one hundred working hours of the 110th Congress. *(Courtesy of AP Images/Susan Walsh)*

per hour to $7.25 per hour over a period of three years. On January 11, the House overturned President Bush's restrictions limiting the funding of stem cell research, and on January 12, it passed a bill changing how negotiations for the cost of prescription drugs for Medicare recipients is handled. The new bill required that the secretary of Health and Human Services, rather than the insurance companies, negotiate the price of the drugs with the drug manufacturers in order to bring down the price of prescription drugs.

By this time, twenty-two of the first hundred hours had passed. On January 17, the House passed a bill that would cut the interest rate on student loans from 6.8 percent to 3.4 percent over the next five years. The following day, the bill on a new energy policy passed the House. This bill rolled back billions of dollars in tax breaks and subsidies to oil-drilling companies. Instead, that money would be put into a reserve fund for companies willing to do research into alternative sources of energy.

Within one hundred working hours, the House of Representatives had written and passed all six of the bills they had promised in their Democratic agenda prior to the 2006 elections.

In her remarks to Congress after she was sworn in as Speaker, Pelosi had said that the American people were looking to Congress to correct the imbalance between the wealthy and the working class. "Our Founders envisioned a new America driven by optimism, opportunity and strength . . . They envisioned America as a just and good place, as a fair and efficient society, as a source of hope and opportunity for all . . . Now it is our responsibility to carry forth that vision of a new America into the twenty-first century," she said. To address this economic imbalance, the Democrats wanted to roll back the tax cuts the Bush administration had given to the wealthiest Americans.

In the week after her election, Speaker Pelosi returned to Baltimore, the city where she had grown up and where her political career had began. In her Little Italy neighborhood, red, white, and green flags, the flags of Italy, fluttered in the breeze. Pelosi visited the statue of her father that the city had erected and laid a bouquet of white roses there. She saw her brother, Tommy, the former mayor, who still lived in Baltimore.

A temporary stage had been erected in front of the house in which she grew up. The entire neighborhood, including

Pelosi approaches a statue of her father while in Baltimore to attend a celebration in her honor. *(Courtesy of AP Images/Chris Gardner)*

longtime residents who had known her when she was called "Little Nancy," turned out to greet her. After being introduced by her brother, Pelosi told the well-wishers, "I wanted to come back here to say thank you to all of you, for the spirit of community that has always strengthened and inspired my life. Every step that I took to the speakership began in this neighborhood." The mayor of Baltimore responded by renaming the block "Little Nancy" grew up on *Via Nancy D'Alesandro Pelosi.*

Pelosi returned to Washington and continued to hammer away at President Bush's Iraq policy. It was rumored that the president had a new plan for the war that would include sending as many as 20,000 additional troops to Iraq. Pelosi hinted that the Democrats would deny Bush the ability to wage a war without end, thereby denying the administration the funds to continue funding the war. "The American people and the Congress support those troops," she said. "We will not abandon them. But if the president wants to add to this mission, he is going to have to justify it and this is new for him because up until now the Republican Congress has given him a blank check with no oversight, no standards, no conditions." She implied that, with the new Democrat-controlled Congress, that was about to change.

The House Armed Services Committee drafted a bill that would address the Democrats' concerns about the war in Iraq. The bill made its way out of committee and was debated on the floor of the House. Many members wanted to vote for the bill, but did not want it to include a specific date for withdrawing troops. "The American people have lost faith in the president's conduct of this war," Pelosi said when the debate ended. "The American people see the reality of the war; the president does not."

On March 23, the House voted to pass the bill by a slim margin of 218-212. It set a timetable for bringing the troops home from Iraq. The bill called for a gradual troop reduction as the Iraqis take on increased responsibility for the security of their own country. It required that most American troops be removed from Iraq by September 2008. The bill also included money to fund the wars in Iraq and Afghanistan.

The vote was strictly along party lines. The Democrats voted for the bill; all but two Republicans in the House voted against it. A week later, the Senate voted on their own version of a bill to bring the troops home from Iraq. Their bill, which they passed, called for most troops to come home by March 2008.

Even though the separate bills passed, many members were fearful of what would happen to Iraq if American troops were withdrawn. Republicans in both houses of Congress (and those Democrats who voted against the bills) felt that it would be a disaster for the Iraqi government and the Iraqi people if U.S. troops left. The Iraqi government was not ready to govern without help from the United States and its allies, they said.

The House and the Senate needed to come up with a single compromise bill. After both houses of Congress voted on the compromise bill, it would be sent to the president for his signature. But President Bush had already said that he would veto a bill calling for a timetable for withdrawal of troops. It would take two-thirds of each house to override the veto, and both the House and Senate were fairly certain they did not have that majority.

At the end of April, a compromise bill, which passed both houses of Congress, was sent to President Bush. It called for troops to begin leaving Iraq on October 1, 2007, and be completely out of that country six months later.

As he had promised, Bush vetoed the bill. Nancy Pelosi and other congressional leaders met with the president, then returned to the House to vote again in an attempt to override the veto. The vote was 222-203, sixty-two votes short of the two-thirds needed. As it had been originally, the vote was strictly along party lines—220 Democrats and two Republicans voted to override; 203, mostly Republicans, voted against overriding the president's veto.

House Democratic leaders after passing the Iraq Accountability Act

It was back to the drawing boards in the House to draft a revised bill that would keep the timetable, but one that the president would sign. He continued to insist that he would veto any bill that contained a timetable, but seemed agreeable to signing a bill that contained benchmarks, or goals, to be achieved by the Iraqi government. The goals included an agreement among the Shiite, Sunni, and Kurdish factions on how they would share the money earned from Iraq's huge oil fields, create jobs that would help to rebuild the country, and hold regional and local elections.

The question remained: Would the Democrats give in and give President Bush the bill he wanted, one without a timetable for withdrawal of American troops from Iraq? Or, would the president prevail and get a bill that did not include a timetable?

"Little Nancy" was once again in the midst of a campaign. But this one was not a campaign to elect a candidate. This one was being waged in order to fulfill a promise to the American people.

Timeline

1940 Born Nancy Patricia D'Alesandro on March 26 in
Baltimore, Maryland.

1946 Begins school at St. Leo's Roman Catholic Church.

1954 Graduates from St. Leo's; begins high school at
all-girls' Institute of Notre Dame.

1958 Enrolls in Trinity College in Washington, D.C.,
after graduation from high school.

1962 Graduates from Trinity College.

1963 Marries Paul Pelosi and moves to New York.

1964 First child, Nancy Corrine, is born.

1966 Daughter Christine is born.

1967 Daughter Jacqueline is born.

1969 Son, Paul Jr., is born; family moves to San Francisco.

1970 Daughter Alexandra is born; begins volunteer work
for the Democratic Party.

1976 Becomes Democratic National Chairwoman
from California for the Democratic National Committee.

1977 Serves as northern chairwoman for the California National Democratic Party.

1981 Appointed state chairwoman for the California National Democratic Party.

1984 Becomes chairwoman of the Democratic National Committee.

1987 Representative Sala Burton of San Francisco dies while in office; elected to finish Burton's term.

1987 Father, Thomas D'Alesandro, dies in Baltimore.

1988 Runs for reelection to the House of Representatives and wins.

1995 Introduces a bill to establish Presidio Trust to provide funding for Presidio National Park in San Francisco; mother, Nancy D'Alesandro, dies in Baltimore.

2002 Becomes House Minority Whip in January; becomes House Minority Leader in November.

2007 Elected Speaker of the House of Representatives.

Sources

CHAPTER ONE: A Noble Calling

p. 13, "This is an historic moment . . ." John M. Broder, "Making History, Pelosi Rises to Speaker," *New York Times*, January 5, 2007.

p. 14-15, "He thinks . . ." Marc Sandalow and Erin McCormick, "Pelosi's goal: Democrats back on top," *San Francisco Chronicle*, April 2, 2006.

p. 15, "It's not where you live . . ." "The Little World of Tommy," *Time*, April 26, 1954, 29.

p. 19, "During the leaner years . . ." Sandalow and McCormick, "Pelosi's goal: Democrats back on top."

p. 19, "Our whole lives . . ." Mark Z. Barabak, "Triumph of the 'Airhead,'" *Los Angeles Times*, January 26, 2003.

p. 19, "our lives were about . . ." Adam Clymer, "A New Vote Counter—Nancy Patricia Pelosi," *New York Times*, October 11, 2001.

p. 19-20, "We'd call people up . . ." Sandalow and McCormick, "Pelosi's goal: Democrats back on top."

p. 20, "I was pampered . . ." Nancy Pelosi, "Nancy Pelosi: Two Heartbeats Away," *60 Minutes,* October 22, 2006, http://www.cbsnews.com/stories/206/10/20/60minutes/main2111089.shtm.

p. 20-21, "Let me just say . . ." Peggy Lewis, "Trinity Graduate Nancy Pelosi '62 Makes History as

the First Woman Elected Speaker of the House," http://
www.trinitydc.edu/admissions/profile_pelosi.php.

CHAPTER TWO: Marriage and Family Come First

p. 24, "Well, we end up . . ." Pelosi, "Nancy Pelosi:
Two Heartbeats Away."

p. 24, "We were always expected . . ." Ibid.

p. 24, "We five kids . . ." Sandalow and McCormick,
"Pelosi's goal: Democrats back on top."

p. 26, "We'll use this for fundraising." Harold
Myerson, "Meyerson: Sala's Choice; Nancy Pelosi
Carries on a Powerful Legacy," *Washington Post*,
January 3, 2007.

p. 27, "It was important . . ." Peggy Lewis, "Profile: Nancy
Pelosi '62 House Democratic Leader," http://www.
trinitydc.edu/admissions/profile_pelosi.php.

CHAPTER THREE: Running for Congress

p. 31, "I have never not participated . . ." Barabak,
"Triumph of the 'Airhead.'"

p. 31, "I really believe . . ." Keith Love, "Democrats
Move Gingerly to Seek Burton House Seat," *Los
Angeles Times*, January 25, 1987.

p. 32, "Sala told me . . ." Peggy Simpson, "Nancy Pelosi:
Ms. Woman of the Year 2002," *Ms*, Winter 2002, http://
www.msmagazine.com/dec02/pelosi_full.asp.

p. 34, "What are the issues? . . ." Keith Love, "14
Candidates Head for Wire in S.F.'s 5th District,"
Los Angeles Times, April 6, 1987.

p. 36, "I am very happy . . ." Keith Love and Dan
Morain, "Pelosi Wins Democratic Contest for Burton
Seat," *Los Angeles Times*, April 8, 1987.

p. 37, "I would try . . ." Robert Lindsey, "House Race in

West Goes to Runoff," *New York Times*, April 9, 1
987.

p. 37, "she launches . . ." "Nancy Pelosi Becomes First
Female House Speaker," *NewsHour,* January 2, 2007,
http://pbs.org/newshour/bb/politics/jan-june07/pelosi_01-
02.html.

p. 38, "Nothing was more significant . . ." "Pelosi Wins
Easily in S.F. Congress Race," *Los Angeles Times*,
June 3, 1987.

p. 38, "My top priorities . . ." Ibid.

CHAPTER FOUR: Representative Pelosi of California

p. 47, "I'm a *paisano* . . ." "Thomas D'Alesandro, 84;
Former Mayor of Baltimore, State Democratic Official,"
Los Angeles Times, August 29, 1987.

p. 49, "This Presidio legislation anticipates . . ." Marc
Sandalow, "California Lawmakers Act to Secure
Presidio Funds," *San Francisco Chronicle*,
March 23, 1995.

p. 49, "She was an incredible woman . . ." "Nancy
D'Alesandro: Nancy Pelosi's mother," San
Francisco Chronicle, April 5, 1995, http://sfgate.com/
cgibin/article.cgi?file=/e/a/1995/04/05/NEWS10478.dtl.

p. 49, "had office hours . . ." Ibid.

p. 49, "My mother was practicing. . ." Ibid.

p. 52, "She is truly a star . . ." Louis Freedberg, "Pelosi
Raises Big War Chest for Democrats," *San
Francisco Chronicle*, October 14, 2000.

p. 52, "Every year, TB . . ." Nancy Pelosi, "Pelosi and
Kerry Introduce Legislation to Provide Incentives for
Research on Vaccines," news release, March 1, 2000,
http://www.house.gov/pelosi/prinfect.htm.

CHAPTER FIVE: House Minority Whip

p. 55, "promote diversity . . ." Adam Clymer, "Two Competing for Post of Democratic Whip in the House," *New York Times*, October 10, 2001.

p. 55, "The idea of right-left . . ." Ibid.

p. 56-57, "Mr. Speaker . . ." "Tribute to Nancy Pelosi," 107th Cong., 1st. sess., *Congressional Record*, Vol. 148, (February 5, 2002): H131.

p. 57, "Mr. Speaker, as we . . ." "Congratulations for the Honorable Nancy Pelosi, Member of Congress, New Minority Whip," 107th Cong., 1st sess., *Congressional Record*, Vol. 148, (February 5, 2002): H126-H127.

p. 57-58, "Nancy, congratulations . . ." Ibid.

p. 59, "We must assist New York . . ." Adam Clymer, "A New Vote Counter—Nancy Patricia Pelosi," *New York Times*, October 11, 2001.

p. 59, "Can we conclude . . ." Bob Woodward, *Plan of Attack* (New York: Simon & Schuster, 2004), 307.

p. 60, "We must protect . . ." Micah L. Sifry and Christopher Cerf, ed., *The Iraq War Reader* (New York: Touchstone/Simon & Schuster, 2003), 262-263.

p. 60, "I have seen no evidence . . ." "Nancy Pelosi Fights to Lead the Democrats," *The Nation*, November 7, 2002, http://www.thenation.com/blogs/thebeat?pid=149.

p. 61-62, "I think the president . . ." Nancy Pelosi, interview by Robert Novak and Al Hunt, *CNN Evans, Novak, Hunt & Shields,* February 16, 2002, http://cnnstudentnews.cnn.com/TRANSCRIPTS/0202/16/en.00.html.

p. 62, "do nothing . . ." Ibid.

p. 62, "the law . . ." Ibid.

CHAPTER SIX: House Minority Leader

p. 65, "Politics is about motion . . ." Sandalow and McCormick, "Pelosi's goal: Democrats back on top."

p. 67, "I didn't run as a woman . . ." Ellen Guettler, "The 108th Congress: Crisis and Conflicts," PBS, *Online NewsHour,* http://www.pbs.org/newshour/108th/bio_pelosi.html.

p. 67, "Where we . . ." Barabak, "Triumph of the 'Airhead.'"

p. 67-68, "When you raise . . ." Ibid.

p. 69, "Our plans . . ." "The 108th Congress: Crisis and Conflicts—Rep. Nancy Pelosi," interview by Ray Suarez, *Online NewsHour*, PBS, January 28, 2003, http://pbs.org/newshour/bb/congress/jan_june03/108th_pelosi_1-28.html.

p. 69-70, "Our children deserve . . ." Nancy Pelosi, "Pelosi Receives 2003 Environmental Leadership Award from California League of Conservation Voters," news release, California League of Conservation Voters, June 16, 2003, http://www.house.gov/pelosi/prEnviroLeadershipAward061603.htm.

p. 70-71, "Sadly, others . . ." Ibid.

p. 71, "People try to instill . . ." Barabak, *Los Angeles Times*, January 26, 2003.

p. 71, "We're on a course . . ." Nancy Pelosi, interview by Tim Russert, *NBC News' Meet the Press*, NBC, May 30, 2004, http://www.msnbc.msn.com/id/5086094/.

p. 71-72, "Bush is an incompetent leader . . ." Ibid.

p. 72, "We owe them . . ." Ibid.

p. 74, "The question should be asked . . ." Edward Epstein, "House Democrats urge special session about 9/11," *San Francisco Chronicle*, August 11, 2004.

CHAPTER SEVEN: The Midterm Elections of 2006

p. 77, "I'm not absolutely certain . . ." Susan Saulny, "House Speaker Offers Words of Hope for New Orleans," *New York Times*, March 4, 2006.

p. 78, "I fully intend . . ." Sandalow and McCormick, "Pelosi's goal: Democrats back on top."

p. 79, "Members of Congress . . ." Keith Bradsher, "As Trade Deficit Grows, So Do Tensions With China," *New York Times*, March 10, 2006.

p. 79, "We have to be ready . . ." Jonathan Weisman, "Confident Democrats Lay Out Agenda," *Washington Post*, May 7, 2006.

p. 80, "You never know . . ." Ibid.

p. 81, "In these times . . ." Steven R. Weisman, "Democrats Opening Assault on Bush Security Policies," *New York Times*, March 29, 2006.

p. 84, "It was a thumpin'. . ." "Democrats win control of Senate," *NBC*, *MSNBC* and news services, November 9, 2006, http://www.msnbc.msn. com/id/15620405/.

p. 84-85, "I met with President Bush . . ." Nancy Pelosi, "Rocky Mountain News: New Dem Leader: We Won't Disappoint," November 13, 2006, http://speaker.gov/ newsroom/articles?id=0001.

p. 85, "But nowhere was the call . . ." "Pelosi ready for House helm, battle over issues," commentary by Eliott C. McLaughlin, *CNN*, November 9, 2006, http://www.cnn.com/2006/POLITICS/11/08/pelosi. speaker/index.html.

p. 85, "The president's acceptance . . ." Nancy Pelosi, "Rocky Mountain News: New Dem Leader: We Won't Disappoint."

p. 85-86, "We certainly have a mandate . . ." "Democrats

win control of Senate," *NBC*, *MSNBC* and news services.

CHAPTER EIGHT: A New Direction for America

p. 80, "In a few moments . . ." Jonathan Weisman and Shailagh Murray, "New Speaker Pelosi Shepherds Ethics Bills to Passage in House," *Washington Post*, January 5, 2007.

p. 88, "I accept this gavel . . ." Nancy Pelosi's opening remarks to Congress, January 4, 2007, http://speaker. gov/newsroom/peeches?id=0006.

p. 90, "The American people . . ." John M. Broder, "Making History, Pelosi Rises to Speaker," *New York Times*, January 5, 2007.

p. 90-91, "It is the responsibility . . ." Ibid.

p. 93, "Our Founders envisioned . . ." Nancy Pelosi, "Pelosi Calls for a New America, Built on the Values that Made Our Country Great," (speech to 110th Congress, January 4, 2007).

p. 94, "I wanted to come back . . ." Matthew Hay Brown, "Baltimore Sun: All Signs Point to Home; House Speaker Nancy Pelosi is honored in Little Italy, where she grew up, with a street named after her," January 6, 2007, http://speaker.gov/newsroom/ articles?id=0004.

p. 95, "The American people . . ." "Pelosi: No Blank Check For Bush In Iraq," *CBS*, "Face the Nation," January 7, 2007, http://www.cbsnews.com/stories/2007/01/07/ ftn/main2335193.shtml" \l "ccmm.

p. 95, "The American people have . . ." Jeff Zeleny, "House, 218 to 212, Votes to Set Date for Iraq Pullout," *New York Times*, March 24, 2007.

Bibliography

Argersinger, Jo Ann E. *Toward a New Deal in Baltimore: People and Government in the Great Depression.* Chapel Hill, North Carolina: The University of North Carolina Press, 1988.

Barilleaux, Ryan J., and Mark J. Rozell. *Power and Prudence: The Presidency of George H.W. Bush.* College Station, Texas: Texas A&M University Press, 2004.

Christianson, Stephen G. *Facts About the Congress.* New York: The H.W. Wilson Company, 1996.

Clinton, Bill. *My Life.* New York: Vintage Books, 2005.

Dallek, Robert. *An Unfinished Life: John F. Kennedy (1917-1963).* New York: Little, Brown and Company, 2003.

Deleon, Richard Edward. *Left Coast City: Progressive Politics in San Francisco, 1975-1991.* Lawrence, Kansas: University Press of Kansas, 1992.

Durr, Kenneth D. *Behind the Backlash: White Working-Class Politics in Baltimore, 1940-1980.* Chapel Hill, North Carolina: The University of North Carolina Press, 2003.

Fitzgerald, Frances. *Way Out There in the Blue: Reagan, Star Wars and the End of the Cold War.* New York: Simon & Schuster, 2000.

Keegan, John. *The Iraq War.* New York: Alfred A. Knopf, 2004.

Kennedy, John F. *Profiles in Courage*. New York: HarperCollins, 2003.

Mann, James. *About Face: A History of America's Curious Relationship with China, from Nixon to Clinton*. New York: Alfred A. Knopf, Inc., 1998.

Mylroie, Laurie. *The War Against America: Saddam Hussein and the World Trade Center Attacks*. New York: ReganBooks, 2001.

Olson, Sherry H. *Baltimore: The Building of an American City*. Baltimore, Maryland: The Johns Hopkins University Press, 1999.

Palmer, Barbara, and Dennis Simon. *Breaking the Political Glass Ceiling: Women and Congressional Elections*. New York: Routledge/Taylor & Francis Group, LLC, 2006.

Pemberton, William E. *Exit with Honor: The Life and Presidency of Ronald Reagan*. Armonk, New York: M.E. Sharpe, Inc., 1997.

Shawcross, William. *Allies: The U.S., Britain, Europe, and the War in Iraq*. New York: PublicAffairs/Perseus Books Group, 2004.

Star, John Bryan. Understanding China: *A Guide to China's Economy, History, and Political Structure*. New York: Hill and Wang, 1997.

Witcover, Jules. *Party of the People: A History of the Democrats*. New York: Random House, 2003.

Web Sites

http://www.democrats.org/
The official Web site of the Democratic Party.

http://www.house.gov
The official Web site of the House of Representatives.

http://www.speaker.house.gov
Articles, a brief biography, and press releases about Nancy Pelosi can be found at this official Web site of the Speaker of the House.

Index